TRANSPORTATION IN MY COMMUNITY

BUSES

by Cari Meister

PEBBLE
a capstone imprint

Beep! Beep!

Buses take us here.
They take us there.

Buses take us everywhere!

It's almost time for school.
Hop on the school bus.

A school bus is big and yellow. It has flashing lights and a red sign that tell cars to **STOP!**

Let's go to the museum downtown.
We'll take a city bus.

Check the bus routes.
Which bus should we take?

Want to explore a city in another state?

Climb aboard a coach bus.
A coach is comfortable.

It has soft seats and big windows.
Some have TVs and bathrooms.

Are you in a band?
You need a tour bus!

Decorate it before you hit the road.

A double decker bus has two levels of seats.
It can carry more passengers than regular buses.

Ride on the bottom level if you want to exit quickly. If you want a good view, ride up top!

Buses take you where you want to go.
How do they work?

A bus has an engine.
It's the machine that powers the bus.

Sometimes the engine is up front.
Or it could be in the back.

A bus has a big steering wheel.
It turns the bus right and left.

The bus's headlights help the driver see in darkness and bad weather.

The signal lights tell other cars when the bus is turning.

Air brakes help buses stop easier. When the driver steps on the brake pedal, air is released.

A bus has many seats and windows.
There are racks to store your things.

The bus comes to a stop.
It's time to get off the bus.
The bus driver opens the door with a lever.

Out you go!

All kinds of buses fill the roads
today—from double deckers to city buses.

But what were the first buses like?

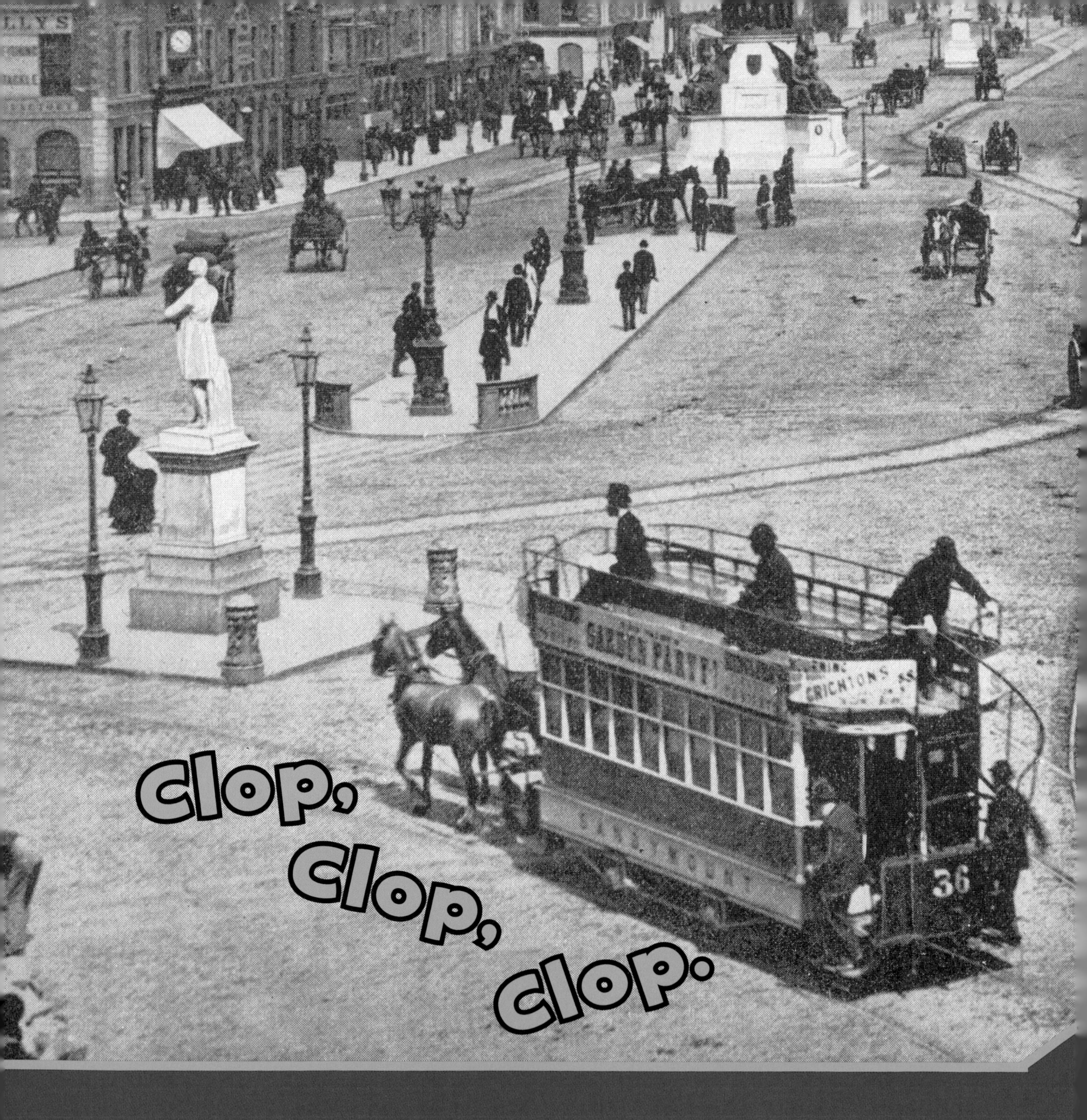

Clop,
Clop,
Clop.

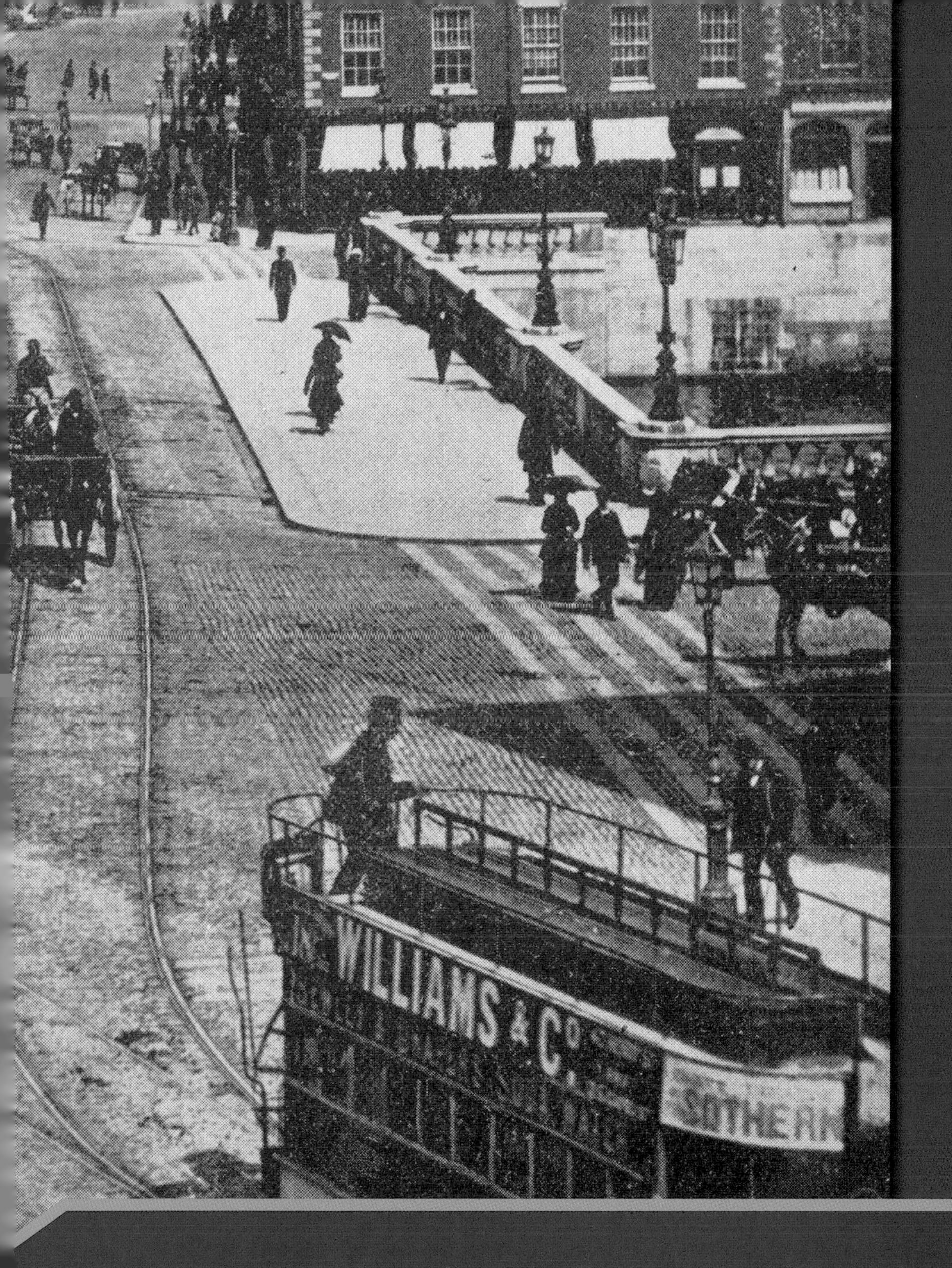

Before buses, there were horse-buses.
Up to 16 people could ride inside.
The driver sat outside to steer the horses.

Soon motor-powered buses appeared on city streets.

These buses were built like trucks.
They had tall frames and diesel engines.

Today engineers are designing new buses. Someday buses will not have drivers! Self-driving buses are already being tested.

What do you think buses will look like in the future?

Timeline

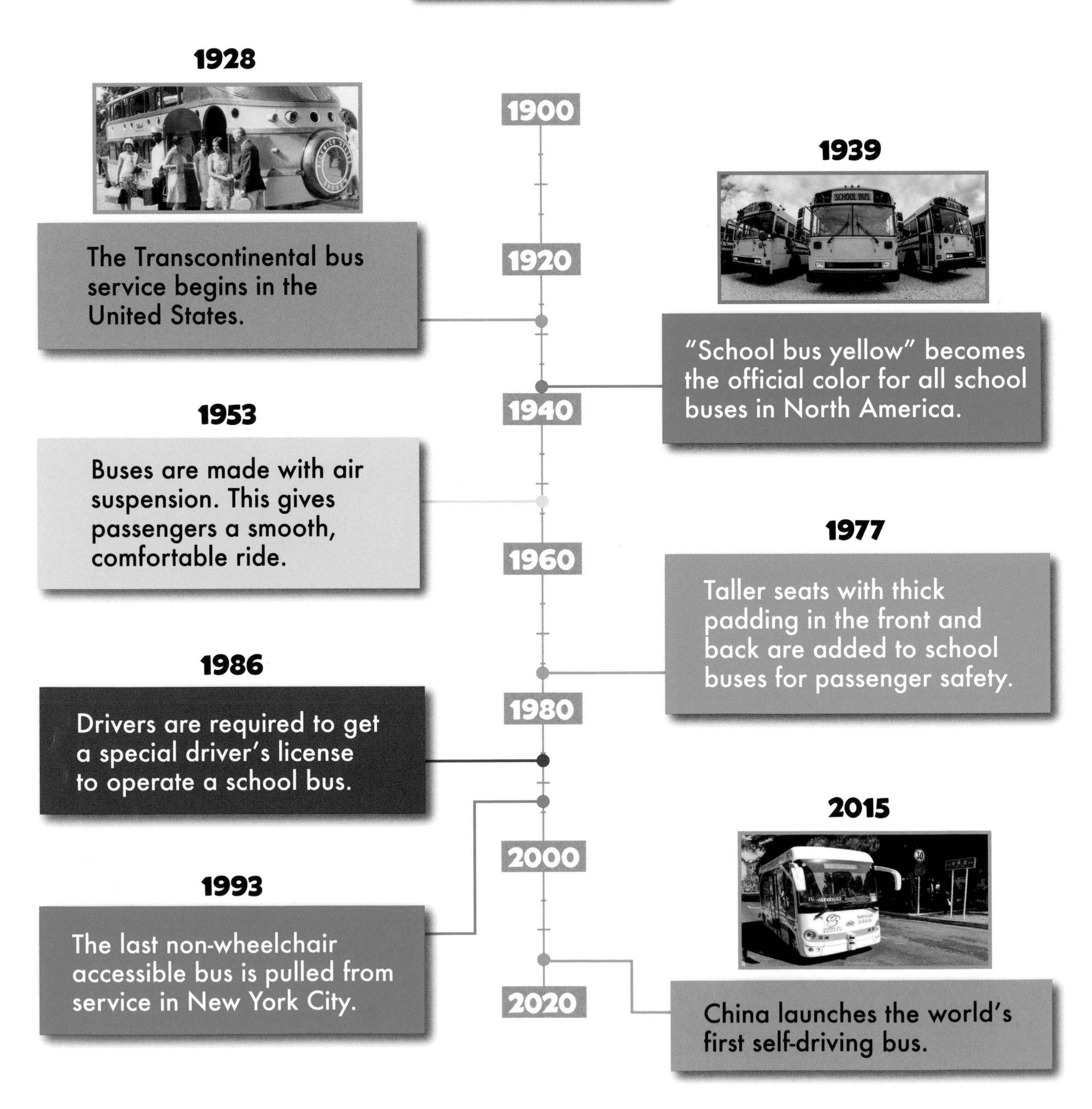
1928
The Transcontinental bus service begins in the United States.
1939
"School bus yellow" becomes the official color for all school buses in North America.
1953
Buses are made with air suspension. This gives passengers a smooth, comfortable ride.
1977
Taller seats with thick padding in the front and back are added to school buses for passenger safety.
1986
Drivers are required to get a special driver's license to operate a school bus.
1993
The last non-wheelchair accessible bus is pulled from service in New York City.
2015
China launches the world's first self-driving bus.
1900
1920
1940
1960
1980
2000
2020
SCHOOL BUS

Glossary

air brake (AYR BRAYK)—a brake that uses air pressure to stop the vehicle

engine (EN-juhn)—a machine that makes the power needed to move something

engineer (en-uhn-NEER)—someone trained to design and build machines and vehicles

lever (LEV-ur)—a bar or a handle that you use to work or control a machine

route (ROUT)—the roads and stops a bus takes

suspension (suh-SPEN-shuhn)—the system of springs and other parts that absorb a bus's movements so the ride is more comfortable

transcontinental (transs-kon-tuh-NEN-tuhl)—crossing a continent

Read More

Lyons, Shelly. *Transportation in My Neighborhood.* My Neighborhood. North Mankato, MN: Capstone Press, 2013.

Reinke, Beth Bence. *School Buses on the Go.* Machines that Go. Minneapolis: Lerner Publications, 2018.

Summers, Alex. *School Bus.* Transportation and Me! Vero Beach, FL: Rourke Educational Media, 2016.

Internet Sites

Use FactHound to find Internet sites related to this book.

Visit *www.facthound.com*

Just type in 9781977106810 and go.

Check out projects, games and lots more at **www.capstonekids.com**

Index

A+ Books are published by Pebble,
1710 Roe Crest Drive, North Mankato, Minnesota 56003
www.mycapstone.com

Library of Congress Cataloging-in-Publication Data
Library of Congress Cataloging-in-publication data is available on the Library of Congress website.
ISBN: 978-1-9771-0681-0 (library binding)
ISBN: 978-1-9771-0682-7 (paperback)
ISBN: 978-1-9771-0683-4 (eBook PDF)

Editorial Credits
Michelle Parkin, editor; Rachel Tesch, designer; Heather Mauldin, media researcher; Katy LaVigne, production specialist

Photo Credits
Alamy: Robert Davis, 10-11; Dreamstime: Sonya Etchison, 18; Getty Images: George Rinhart/Corbis, 30 (top left), Universal History Archive/UIG, 26-27, VCG, 30 (bottom right); iStockphoto: alexmak72427, 20, anouchka, 13, bauhaus1000, 24-25, DarthArt, 17, gerenme, 19, kali9, 21, manonallard, 5, matt_dela, 8-9, narvikk, 22-23, Tramino, 29; Shutterstock: Allard One, 30 (top right), Dmitri Ma, 9 (inset), DW labs Incorporated, 7, Joe Ravi, cover (bottom right), Krivosheev Vitaly, cover (bottom middle), Mike Focus, cover (top), 1, Milos Muller, 14-15, Monkey Business Images, 4, photopixel, cover (bottom left), Rawpixel.com, 6, Savo Ilic, 15 (inset), S-F, 12, Sorbis, 16, TRAIMAK, 28, visualgang, 2-3

Printed and bound in the United States of America.
PA49